Come Write With Me:

POETRY

Workbook & Journal

Brooke E. Wayne

For
TEENS
&
ADULTS
Volume 1

Hearts & Flowers

Publishing

Contact the author at www.brookeewayne.com.

ISBN: 9781734163704
Imprint: 1734163704

Chief Editor: Anette Blaskovich

Title: Come Write with Me: POETRY Workbook & Journal (For Teens & Adults)
Author: Brooke E. Wayne
Publisher: Hearts & Flowers Publishing
Excerpts: Public Domain and Author's permission
Cover Photo: Shuttershock
Font: American Typewriter
Graphics: Pixabay.com, PublicDomainVectors.com (Free Stock Photos for Publication)

Description: A workbook loaded with creative writing tools to compose poetry, including fill-ins, worksheets, examples, structured writing exercises, unstructured journal space, and much more!

Category: Creative Writing Workbook, Creative Writing Journal, Poetry Workbook, Poetry Journal, Creative Writing Prompts, Poetry Writing Prompts, Poetry Starters, Creative Writing Starters, Poetry Lessons, Creative Writing Lessons, Structured Creative Writing, Instructional Workbook, Standards-based Learning, Homeschool Workbook, ELA Workbook, English Language Arts Curriculum

A Special Thank You to...

Anette Blaskovich thank you for your eye for detail and constant support.

Robin Woods thank you for contributing original haiku poetry, as well as your editing expertise. Find more of Robin's writing at www.robinwoodsfiction.com.

TABLE OF CONTENTS

PICTORIAL INSPIRATION 139

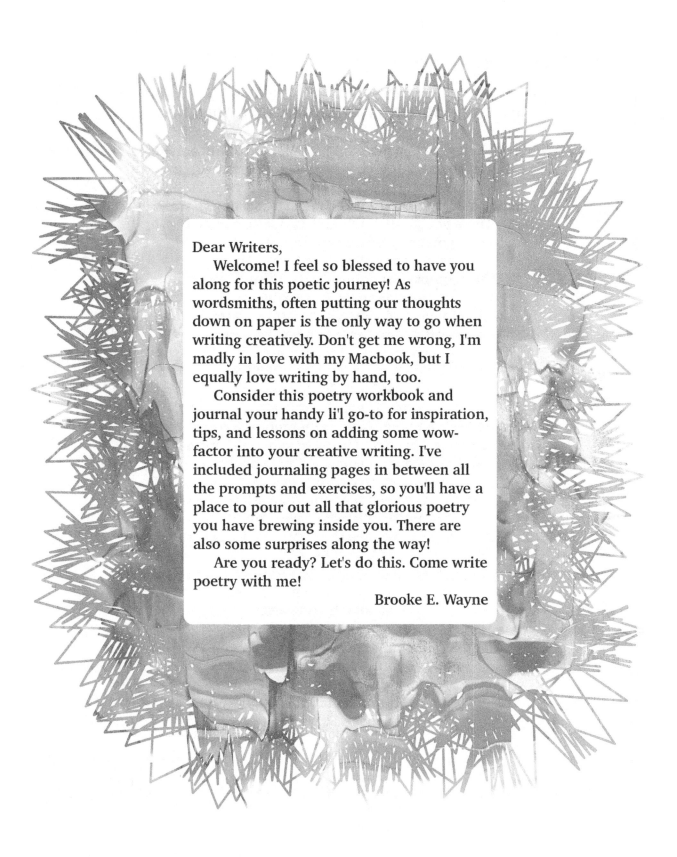

Dear Writers,

Welcome! I feel so blessed to have you along for this poetic journey! As wordsmiths, often putting our thoughts down on paper is the only way to go when writing creatively. Don't get me wrong, I'm madly in love with my Macbook, but I equally love writing by hand, too.

Consider this poetry workbook and journal your handy li'l go-to for inspiration, tips, and lessons on adding some wow-factor into your creative writing. I've included journaling pages in between all the prompts and exercises, so you'll have a place to pour out all that glorious poetry you have brewing inside you. There are also some surprises along the way!

Are you ready? Let's do this. Come write poetry with me!

Brooke E. Wayne

HOW TO USE THIS WORKBOOK AND JOURNAL

We're all bringing our own unique talents to the table here.
Maybe you're a novice writer. Maybe you're a pro.
Either way, the prompts and exercises are meant to inspire,
and the Toolbox section is the perfect place to start.
Once you go through all the poetic devices
polishing up your creative craft,
feel free to skip around after that.
The prompts, structured poems, and lessons
are meant to be flexible.
It's all about you exploring your unlimited imagination.
I want you to become a better writer
when you get to the end of
Come Write with Me: POETRY
Workbook & Journal
(For Teens & Adults).
There's an unspoken unity among writers.
You know this if you've ever ventured online
and hung out on some writerly hashtags
or in some writerly groups.
We are individual voices that come together in harmony.
A unity of souls--if you will.
And I am present to share the love of writing with you.
Okay, whew!
Now that I've gotten all that mushy, serious jargon out of me,
from here on out, be forewarned,
I'm all snark and sass.
There. I said it.
Now, sharpen your pencil,
get your bootie in a chair,
kick up your feet,
and show me what you've got.
~ Brooke E. Wayne

Creative Writing
Toolbox

Hey? Psst. I did a thing.
I made this workbook interactive.
With every lesson in the Toolbox,
I added an extended version
with more prompts and
a full example of the poetic device
in action for you to enjoy.
All you have to do to enhance your
page-turning experience is
click on the QR codes.
No QR scanner? Download a free app.
No cell phone?
You can still go directly to my blog
using a computer:
www.brookeewayne.com
You'll find the treasure trove
of expansions there.
Just hop around my categories
in the box at the bottom of the Home page.
My intention is to make this journey fun!
You're welcome.

LITERARY TERMS

END RHYME-----The ends of two or more lines of poetry rhyme together

FREE VERSE-----A poem that cannot rhyme

FOOT-----A measurement of stressed and unstressed syllables (Syllables are pronounciated word parts: beau-ti-ful has three syllables)

INTERNAL RHYME-----A line of poetry that rhymes in the middle and end of the same line

LYRIC-----A highly musical poem, conveying powerful feelings or glimpsing only a portion of a story

METER-----Counting accented and unaccented syllables in a word or group of words, measured by metrical feet (iamb, trochee, spondee, dactyl, anapest)

NARRATIVE POEM-----A poem that reflects a complete story with a beginning, inciting moment, middle, and end that satisfies the reader (may or may not rhyme)

POETIC DEVICES-----Figurative language used to enhance a poem

RHYME SCHEME-----Alphabetically labeling the end rhymes of a poem, creating a pattern (Example: ABAB CDCD EFEF GG)

RHYTHM-----A pattern of stressed and unstressed beats composed of metrical units

STANZA-----A group of lines in a poem--the way essays have paragraphs, poems have stanzas

VERSE-----A line of poetry

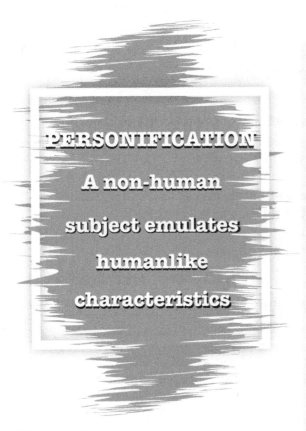

PERSONIFICATION

A non-human subject emulates humanlike characteristics

Dear Writer,

Bringing things that lack a heartbeat to life with the poetic device of personification is like pumping water into a balloon; it goes from,'Oh hey, a balloon! Fun!" to, "Give it to me now! It's mine!" Then, let the scheming begin on who's going to be the recipient of the balloon with a bellyful of water and a wicked mission to drench somebody. The balloon suddenly takes on a life of his own with a story he's dying to tell.

Adding lifelike attributes, action, or feelings to a non-human gives writing character and animation to an otherwise ordinary poem.

Now, underline all the phrases of personification I snuck into this note. I bet the page will growl from being slashed by your pencil!

~Brooke E. Wayne

PROMPTS

Time crawls, life ebbs and flows, steam or smoke curls its fingers, clouds race across the sky, moon peers down, stars blink, trees breathe, moan, or sigh, waves march or trample, sunrays caress or bite, wind snarls or screams, flowers sing or dance, breeze whispers or howls, rainfall tickles or pinches, fear swallows whole, love devours, dreams capture, path beckons or warns, stones cry out, leaves tremble or wave, heat smothers. Also apply pronouns to objects like Car=She, etc.

Hit up the QR Code for some inspiration. Vet through the prompt list or branch out on your own and bring humanlike life to some of your favorite things. Go ahead, Dr. Frankenstein your poetry with some PERSONIFICATION.

I Wandered Lonely as a Cloud
by
William Wordsworth

"I wandered lonely as a cloud
That floats on high o'er Vales and Hills,
When all at once I saw a crowd,
A host of golden Daffodils;
Beside the Lake, beneath the trees,
Fluttering and dancing in the breeze."
(Excerpt)

CLASSIC POET'S CORNER

WRITE

_____

_____

_____

_____

_____

_____

_____

_____

_____

_____

_____

_____

_____

_____

_____

_____

_____

SIMILE

When two uncommon items are compared to each other, often using like or as.

Dear Writer,

Ever notice how similes have a clever way of making us smile? Maybe it's subliminal. It could also be that pesky word everybody makes fun of people for overusing, **like**, all the time--even if that word, and its sidekick, **as**, happen to be the crux of helping this poetic device do its thing.

Let's face it, similes are like little goofy emojis that turn a boring sentence into something with character. Similes bring imagination to the table like a bouquet of hand-picked wild flowers. They're an unexpected, pleasant surprise.

I tossed some 'as' simile phrases at you in the prompts section that you're more than welcome to wrap a poem around like a cozy shawl on a cool night, if the muse strikes you.

~ Brooke E. Wayne

PROMPTS

As chill as a glass of iced tea

As crazy as a car full of clowns

As fresh as a new pair of sneakers

As calm as a placid pond

As delicate as a handcrafted doily

As hard as a diamond

As slow as a line at the post office

As reckless as a runaway train

As velvety as a rose petal

As strong as a clove of garlic

As elegant as Irish lace

A Red, Red Rose
by
Robert Burns

"Oh, my Luve is like a red, red rose,
That's newly sprung in June;
Oh, my Luve is like the melody
That's sweetly played in tune."
(Excerpt)

Hit up the QR Code for inspiration. Play around with SIMILES by making a list of opposing objects. Then, dig deep to think of something that gives the whacky duo common ground. See what you come up with, and wrap one of those witty poems you're so fabulous at creating around your new verse.

CLASSIC POET'S CORNER

WRITE

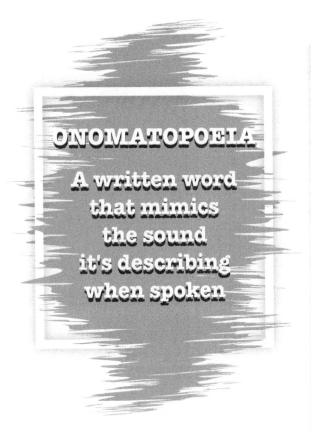

ONOMATOPOEIA

A written word that mimics the sound it's describing when spoken

PROMPTS:

Silly Onomatopoeia:

Squirt, Splish, Bonk, Zoom, Splash, Pop, Boink, Hush, Splat, Eek, Umph, Whoosh, Kaboom, Bong, Zap, Zing

Sensuous Onomatopoeia:

Sing, Swirl, Whisper, Crunch, Hiss, Wimper, Burst, Moan, Whirl, Scream, Rush, Sigh, Gulp, Groan

Hit up the QR code for some inspiration. You can also zoom ahead in this workbook past ONOMATOPOEIA to the word list for IMAGERY in The Sensuous World section. And, of course, feel free to read your work out loud, you fantastic wordsmith you. This device whimpers for attention like that.

Dear Writers,

I don't know about you, but when I think of the device, onomatopoeia, I think of kids trying on poetry for size in early elementary school--lots of 'zoinks' or even a random 'pow' crammed in a line. Many grown-up words produce the sounds they're trying to describe, as well. A word like trickle breathes life into the line, 'a babbling brook trickles over a riverbed of silky smooth rocks' instead of 'goes'. I can hear it, can't you? If you can't resist the urge to scoop up one of those rocks and toss it back into the water with a 'kerplunk', I won't judge, though. Try to squeeze some noisy words into your next poem--silly, if you must.

~Brooke E. Wayne

"The Bells"
by Edgar Allan Poe
I.
"Hear the sledges with the bells--
Silver bells!
What a world of merriment their melody foretells!
How they tinkle, tinkle, tinkle,
In the icy air of night!"
(Excerpt)

CLASSIC POET'S CORNER

WRITE

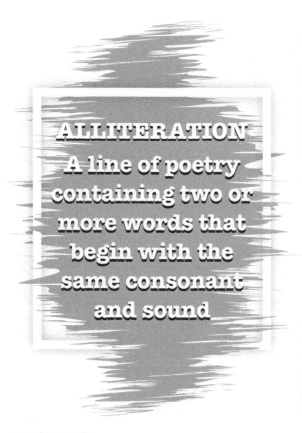

ALLITERATION
A line of poetry containing two or more words that begin with the same consonant and sound

Dear Writer,

We've all rattled off tongue twisters in our childhood at some point or another when we learned about them in school--the way a handful of words could clip off the end of our tongues in a topsy turvy dance of sounds--oh, how exciting those sassy statements could be!

As seemingly juvenile as this simple poetic device is, it may be one of the most powerful tools a poet could use.

It stimulates the reader's intelligence, offering the subconscious an auditory playground to romp around on, even if the reader is only hearing the mellifluous allure of the similar sounding words in his or her head instead of out loud.

Now, circle all the alliteration I packed into this note for practice in recognition.

~ Brooke E. Wayne

PROMPTS

wind, wild, wandering, wish, wistful
heartfelt heavenly, harbinger, hoping
childlike, cherishing, charmed, chilled
beautiful, beguiling, beckon, bright
fanciful, fortitude, fortuitous, fury
dubious, doubtful, determined, dark
besmirch, broken, bereft, bested
special, spectacular, sprite, spirited
precious, pretty, pitiful, perfection
romantic, reminiscent, robust, real
shimmering, shadows, shine, sure
quicken, quivering, quest, quality
tenacious, tentative, timely, task

The Eagle
by
Alfred Lord Tennyson

"He clasps the crag with crooked hands;
Close to the sun in lonely lands,
Ringed with the azure world, he stands."

(Excerpt)

Hit up the QR Code for some inspiration. Use one set of prompt words, use them all, create your own, or mix them up and smash other words in between them, but get it goin' on and load up your glorious poems with ALLITERATION.

CLASSIC POET'S CORNER

WRITE

REPETITION

Repeating a word, phrase, line, stanza, concept, or rhythmical pattern in a poem

Dear Writer,

It's easy to fall into the trap of thinking repetition is simply repeating. That's it. Saying the same 'ol same 'ol over and over, but it's not. It's so much more. Repetition can take on many forms.

Not only is it okay to repeat a part of a poem word for word--songs do it all the time in the form of a chorus--but it's also fine and dandy to repeat a concept in the form of synonyms. Tossing multiple words in a poem that all embody the same meaning counts as repetition.

Stuffing a poem full of like-minded phrases that illustrate the same idea, like a philosophical suggestion, counts, too.

Shakespeare, the one and only lord of sonnet making so much so the English Sonnet changed its name to his, had repetition of rhythm down pat. Behold his addiction to iambic pentameter. (That's ten syllables broken into five pairs of iambic feet with one unstressed syllable followed by a stressed one--aka--baBOOM, baBOOM, baBOOM, baBOOM, baBOOM.)

Go simple or go complex, but, no matter what, just go ahead and go for it.

~ Brooke E. Wayne

PROMPTS:

WORDS: (Think synonyms!)

Happy, Joyful, Jovial, Enthralled
Rage, Frustration, Anger, Aggression
Beautiful, Gorgeous, Pretty, Cute

CONCEPTS: (Let's go existential, shall we?!)

Caged Soul, Body as a Temple,
One with Self, One with God,
Embodying a Spirit, Breath of God,
Seed of Intellect, Soul Chamber

Properly Scholarly Attitude
by
Adelaide Crapsey
"The poet pursues his beautiful theme;
The preacher his golden beatitude;
And I run after a vanishing dream--
The glittering, will-o'-the-wispish gleam
Of the properly scholarly attitude--
The highly desirable, the very advisable,
The hardly acquirable, properly scholarly attitude."
(Excerpt)

Hit up the QR Code for inspiration. REPETITION is not a scapegoat for increasing the length of your poem without any effort. No guilty feelings allowed. This device is all about letting something sink in for the reader—a gentle reminder, if you will. Now, rinse and repeat until your preened poetry is nice and shiny.

CLASSIC POET'S CORNER

WRITE

_____

_____

_____

_____

_____

_____

_____

_____

_____

_____

_____

_____

_____

_____

_____

_____

_____

_____

HYPERBOLE

An absurd exaggeration meant to prove a point

Dear Writer,

Have you ever flipped your lid, busted someone's chops, blown a gasket, or done anything else meriting a goofy idiom to describe your actions?

(Idioms are expressions that have a different context than their literal meaning like being in hot water means you're in trouble with a capital T.)

Imagine if you could bottle up an experience, shake the bejeebies out of it, then pop the top, and let it go. You'd watch in wonder as all the intense feelings and actions explode and bubble over in that moment.

Now imagine describing those feelings with lots of exclamation points and maybe even an eye roll and a tsk, too. Then, go ahead and ramp that moment up again times a million. That's a hyperbole. They're obnoxious exaggerations on redbull and espresso.

Take the meh and turn it into a fierce roar. Because, if you've walked a thousand miles in someone else's shoes or died a thousand deaths to be the one, you might know what I mean when I say, "Blow it up."
~ Brooke E. Wayne

PROMPTS

Turn: happy into ecstatic, fear into trauma, joy into elation, sad into devastated, peace into tranquility, hope into a mission

Go Extreme: millions, forever, a lifetime, neverending, miles, centuries, always, never, best, greatest, most, definite

Story Building: What extreme would you go to for... someone you love, a friend, family, yourself, an enemy, your savior, a stranger, a life-changing cause?

Hit up the QR Code for inspiration. HYPERBOLE have a tendency to make people laugh. The more absurd the punchline, the bigger the guffaws, so keep that in mind when you dive headfirst into your next few fantastic poems.

How Do I Love Thee?
by
Elizabeth Barrett Browning

"How do I love thee?
Let me count the ways.
I love thee
to the depth and breadth and height
my soul can reach,"
(Excerpt Sonnet 43)

CLASSIC POET'S CORNER

WRITE

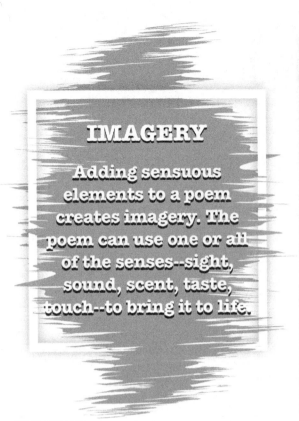

IMAGERY

Adding sensuous elements to a poem creates imagery. The poem can use one or all of the senses--sight, sound, scent, taste, touch--to bring it to life.

PROMPTS

SIGHT:
A bright red barn / sports car/ smiling face / landscape
SOUND:
A ticking clock / bomb / growling / whispered words of love
SCENT:
A pungent dungeon / gym bag / meadow of wild flowers / leather
TASTE:
A succulent peach / wedding cake / street corner hotdog / chilled wine
TOUCH:
A gentle breeze / caress / hot sun / tropical rainfall / holding hands

Hit up the QR Code for some inspiration. Don't feel obligated to bog down your poetry with all the senses--that is, of course, unless you want to. You do you. Add at least one sensory element to every poem. Go forth, you dreamer you, and tap into IMAGERY.

Dear Writer,
   Society, in general, tends to go on and on about how hard it is in life to gush about feelings. We even go so far as to pay PhD holding people to probe into our psyches. We do this with the hope that this professional listener will tap into that fortress of emotions we like to keep under lock and key in our caged hearts and try to make us cry. We then hope to articulate all the why's about those story-holding tears.
   The thing is, it's our job as poem spinners to conjure up the messy feelings in our readers. We are the professional wordsmiths that say all the right words to unlock the readers' hearts. Adding sensuous elements to a poem manifests the vivid, tangible setting that might be needed for the reader to allow any emotions to unfold and do their thing. Create the world they can tap into and actually feel.

                    ~ Brooke E. Wayne

To the Thawing Wind
by
Robert Frost

"Come with rain, O loud Southwester!
Bring the singer, bring the nester;
Give the buried flower a dream;
Make the settled snowbank steam;"

(Excerpt)

CLASSIC POET'S CORNER

WRITE

_____

_____

_____

_____

_____

_____

_____

_____

_____

_____

_____

_____

_____

_____

_____

_____

_____

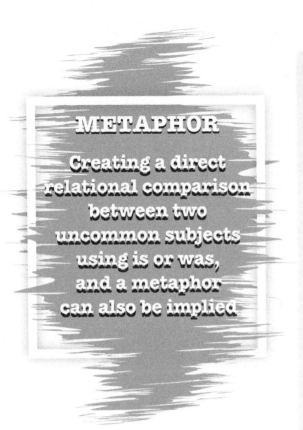

METAPHOR

Creating a direct relational comparison between two uncommon subjects using is or was, and a metaphor can also be implied

Dear Writer,

Metaphors and similes are chatty cousins that hang out and have great conversations about all the things they have in common. For example, they both like to compare stuff 'n' stuff. Metaphors lean in, though, and get directly to the point. Similes, on the other hand, dance around the idea, like, all the time.

Sure, similes have it a little easier when it comes to everyday jargon. Oh, but, metaphors, when given the chance to disguise themselves, can come off as so much more magestic. Implied, even! Forget one-liners, these bad boys show up for the whole enchilada and dominate.

You should dive deep into your writing and anchor your poem with one of these devices!

~Brooke E. Wayne

PROMPTS:

Emotions tied to Objects:

Love .... Anchor, Ocean, Sunshine
Hope .... Wings, Rope, Window
Anger .... Fire Engine, Storm, Hell
Joy .... Buffet, Garden, Rainbow
Sorrow ..... Rainfall, Cloud, Anvil
Fear .... Phantom, Shadow, Train
Anxiety .... Wildfire, Lightning, Claws

Borrow these Implied Metaphor Phrases:

Her smoldering temper was inflamed by the ...
... enveloped by sinking hope.
... smothering them in an ocean of
He shredded the bully with his ...
Their bed of lies ...
The curtain of stars blanketed ...

"'Hope" is the thing with feathers"
by
Emily Dickinson

"'Hope" is the thing with feathers--
That perches in the soul--
And sings the tune without the words--
And never stops--at all--"
(Excerpt)

Hit up the QR code for some inspiration. Hop back over to the Simile section and scratch out the 'as' on the prompts you didn't use, and see what you can wrangle into a solid line of poetic perfection, you curator of clever METAPHORS you.

CLASSIC POET'S CORNER

WRITE

_____

_____

_____

_____

_____

_____

_____

_____

_____

_____

_____

_____

_____

_____

_____

_____

_____

_____

_____

Jack London's Credo is the perfect example of the use of **METAPHOR.** His alleged poem speaks of how he's chosen to live his life to the fullest. (Feel free to jump down the rabbit hole on your own to figure out if he actually penned every word of this poem himself).

We all have an unspoken code we live by. It's time to climb that proverbial mountain of our lives and voice our own credos to the world. I have modeled my personal credo after Jack London's metaphorical masterpiece:

JACK LONDON'S CREDO

I WOULD RATHER BE ASHES THAN DUST!
I WOULD RATHER
THAT MY SPARK SHOULD BURN OUT IN A BRILLIANT BLAZE
THAN IT SHOULD BE STIFLED BY DRY-ROT,
I WOULD RATHER BE A SUPERB METEOR,
EVERY ATOM OF ME IN MAGNIFICENT GLOW,
THAN A SLEEPY AND PERMANENT PLANET.
THE FUNCTION OF MAN IS TO LIVE, NOT TO EXIST.
I SHALL NOT WASTE MY DAYS IN TRYING TO PROLONG THEM.
I SHALL USE MY TIME.

Brooke E. Wayne's Credo

I would rather be a raging ocean than a stagnant lake.
I would rather that my shimmering waves toss ancient grains of sand all day
Than sit lifelessly, awaiting a pebble to shatter my stillness.
I would rather be a hurricane, hurling my salty fury onto land,
shredding everything in my path with a single wave,
Than to be a passive raindrop searching to belong in the sea.
The function of a soul is to thrive, not wait in boredom.
I shall not blend in like a meaningless droplet.
I shall become a tsunami and reign magnificently.

Now, use your voice to write your life's metaphorical CREDO.

CREDO

I would rather be _____

I would rather that _____

than_____

I would rather be _____

_____

than _____

The function of _____

_____

I shall not _____

I shall _____

_____

_____

_____

_____

_____

_____

_____

_____

_____

_____

_____

_____

_____

_____

_____

_____

_____

_____

_____

The
Sensuous
World

Hey? Psst. I used to do a thing.
Once upon a time, during my middle school days, (circa early 1980s),
Confession time ... I had a crush on Ponyboy.
Yep. You know that fictitious dude in
S. E. Hinton's 1960s teenage literary masterpiece The Outsiders
we've all read thanks to English teachers around the world.
Ponyboy was my first book boyfriend.
The movie version, courtesy of Francis Ford Coppola,
had also just come out on HBO, so I was also able to watch the movie
over and over, absorbing all of its wisdom
my thirteen-year-old head could hold.
My biggest take-away ... stop and watch the sunrise--or sunset.
Turns out, it can do wonders for the soul.
It became the 'stop and smell the roses' anthem in my young life.
I put it to practice every morning all the way through high school.
If I wasn't sitting at the dining room table, breakfast drink in hand,
watching the ribbons of peach and powder pink wind their way
through the sapphire sky as the sun edged away the darkness,
I was parked on a hill, sitting on my car's hood, watching that same sun
slowly slip away, leaving tangerine and fuchsia in its wake
like paint swipes on a tree-lined canvas.
What did I get out of sun-watching?
Serenity. Mindfulness. Hope. Closer to God. Closer to me.
Flash forward, and I've spent the last 24 years teaching The Outsiders
and encouraging teens to seek out a little reprieve with the sun.
Talk about a full (sun-shaped) circle in my life. Wow!
Just thought I'd share that with you.
That's all.

IMAGERY

SIGHT	SOUND	TASTE	TOUCH	SCENT
All Colors	Onomatopoeia	Acidic	Abrasive	Aromatic
All Sizes	Barking	Acrid	Bristly	Briny
Bold	Breathy	Bitter	Bumpy	Burnt
Bright	Buzzing	Bittersweet	Clammy	Citrusy
Brilliant	Clanking	Bland	Cold	Dank
Cluttered	Clomping	Buttery	Creamy	Dusty
Curled	Croaky	Chalky	Doughy	Earthy
Curved	Crispy	Chocolaty	Fluffy	Fishy
Dark	Crunchy	Fresh	Furry	Floral
Dim	Dripping	Fruity	Humid	Foul
Dingy	Gong	Honeyed	Greasy	Fragrant
Dull	Groan	Lemony	Grimy	Full-bodied
Faded	Gurgle	Metallic	Gritty	Gamy
Foggy	Gutteral	Minty	Hairy	Garlicky
Glittery	Hoarse	Nutty	Hot	Herbal
Gloomy	Hiss	Raw	Icy	Malted
Glossy	Huff	Resfreshing	Jellied	Metallic
Hazy	Husky	Rich	Leathery	Moldy
Illuminating	Moan	Ripe	Liquid	Musty
Illustrious	Murmur	Roasted	Mushy	Peppery
Iridescent	Peep	Robust	Oily	Perfumed
Milky	Purring	Rotten	Powdery	Piney
Misty	Ringing	Salty	Prickly	Pungent
Murky	Rustle	Savory	Rough	Putrid
Pale	Shrilling	Smoked	Sandy	Rancid
Shabby	Sizzle	Soupy	Satiny	Rank
Shimmering	Slur	Sour	Scalding	Rotten
Shiny	Snivel	Spicy	Silky	Salty
Smudged	Strangled	Stale	Slick	Seasoned
Sparkling	Swoosh	Succulent	Soft	Smoky
Spotted	Thud	Sugary	Stiff	Spiced
Speckled	Thumping	Sweet	Smooth	Spoiled
Straight	Tinkling	Syrupy	Sticky	Sulfuric
Wizened	Trickling	Tangy	Sultry	Stinky
Worn	Whisper	Tart	Velvety	Woodsy

REDS	ORANGES	YELLOWS	GREENS
Amaranth	Amber	Almond	Algae
Baby Pink	Apricot	Banana	Apple
Beet	Auburn	Beige	Army
Berry	Begonia	Biscotti	Avocado
Blood	Bird of Paradise	Bisque	Basil
Blush	Bronze	Blond	Celadon
Bordeaux	Burnt	Brass	Celery
Brick	Cantaloupe	Buff	Chartreuse
Bubblegum	Carrot	Buttercup	Chayote
Burgundy	Cheddar	Buttermilk	Citron
Cabernet	Chrysanthemum	Butternut	Clover
Candy Apple	Cider	Butterscotch	Crocodile
Cardinal	Cinnabar	Camel	Emerald
Carnation	Clementine	Canary	Evergreen
Cayenne	Copper	Candlelight	Forest
Cerise	Coral	Champagne	Grass
Cherry	Creamsicle	Cheesecake	Grasshopper
Chili	Fire	Citrine	Honeydew
Cinnamon	Flame	Corn	Hunter
Claret	Fox	Cream	Jade
Cotton Candy	Ginger	Curry	Juniper
Cranberry	Lava	Custard	Kelly
Crimson	Mandarin	Daffodil	Khaki
Currant	Mango	Daisy	Kiwi
Dragonfruit	Marigold	Dandelion	Laurel
Fire Engine	Marmalade	Dijon	Leaf
Flamingo	Melon	Ecru	Lettuce
Garnet	Navel	Flaxen	Lime
Hot Pink	Orangutan	Gold	Margarita
Lipstick	Papaya	Goldenrod	Mint
Magenta	Peach	Harvest	Mint Julep
Maroon	Persimmon	Honey	Mistletoe
Mauve	Poppy	Honeysuckle	Moss
Paprika	Pumpkin	Lemon	Olive
Pomegranate	Russet	Mustard	Pea
Punch	Rust	Nude	Pea Soup
Raspberry	Saffron	Oatmeal	Peridot
Rose	Salamander	Ochre	Pickle
Rouge	Salmon	Pear	Pine
Ruby	Sherbet	Pearl	Pistachio
Ruddy	Sienna	Pineapple	Sage
Sangria	Spice	Sand	Sea Glass
Scarlet	Squash	Shortbread	Seaweed
Strawberry	Sulfur	Sunflower	Spring
Tea Rose	Sunset	Straw	Spruce
Tomato	Tangerine	Tan	Green Tea
Watermelon	Terra Cotta	Tawny	Teal
Wine	Tiger	Topaz	Tourmaline
Vermilion	Titian	Tuscany	Willow
Vixen	Yam	Vintage	Wintergreen

BLUES

Admiral
Aegean
Aqua
Aquamarine
Azure
Baby Blue
Blue Bell
Blueberry
British
Cadet
Capri
Caribbean
Celestial
Cerulean
Cobalt
Cornflower
Cyan
Delphinium
Denim
Egyptian
Electric
Forget-Me-Not
Geranium
Hyacinth
Imperial
Indigo
Iris
Lagoon
Lake
Lapis
Larimar
Midnight
Navy
Ocean
Oxford
Peacock
Persian
Powder
Robin's Egg
Royal
Sapphire
Sea Foam
Sky
Slate blue
Teal
Tiffany
Topaz
Tropical
Turquoise
Ultramarine

PURPLES

Amethyst
Blackberry
Boysenberry
Byzantine
Concord
Eggplant
Grape
Heather
Hibiscus
Hydrangea
Lavender
Lilac
Merlot
Mulberry
Orchid
Periwinkle
Plum
Violet
Wisteria

WHITES

Alabaster
Antique
Ash
Bone
Cloud
Crystal
Diamond
Dove
Eggshell
Frost
Ice
Ivory
Lace
Marble
Marshmallow
Mist
Opal
Oyster
Paper
Parchment
Pearl
Platinum
Porcelain
Silver
Snow
Sugar
Vanilla

BROWNS

Beige
Birch
Brunette
Cappuccino
Caramel
Cedar
Chestnut
Chocolate
Coffee
Fawn
Hazelnut
Hickory
Leather
Mahogany
Mocha
Nutmeg
Oak
Pecan
Russet
Sand
Sandalwood
Sandstone
Sepia
Tan
Toffee
Redwood
Rust
Walnut
Wheat

BLACKS

Charcoal
Ebony
Granite
Graphite
Gray
Gun Metal
Ink
Jet
Obsidian
Onyx
Pewter
Pitch
Sable
Smoke
Soot
Steel
Stone

YOUR LIST

_____
_____
_____
_____
_____
_____
_____
_____
_____
_____
_____
_____
_____
_____
_____
_____
_____
_____
_____
_____
_____
_____
_____
_____
_____
_____
_____
_____
_____
_____
_____
_____
_____
_____

BRAINSTORM EXAMPLE

Choose a SUNRISE or SUNSET:
(Sun rises in the east, Sun sets in the west)

sunset

Choose a SEASON:
(Spring, Summer, Autumn, Winter)

summer

What do you SEE?

waves, sand, shells, palm trees, dolphins, clouds, colors in the sky
colors on the water

What do you HEAR?

waves crashing, sea gulls squawking, sizzling sun
palm leaves rustling

What do you SMELL?

salty breeze, coconut suntan lotion

What do you TASTE?

salty sea water, strawberry ice cream

What do you TOUCH?

gritty sand between my toes, scorching sunrays
warm water, crisp breeze, sunburned skin

How does this image make you FEEL?

happy, joyful, relaxed, lazy, peaceful, calm, tranquil, worn out

BRAINSTORM

Choose a SUNRISE or SUNSET:
(Sun rises in the east, Sun sets in the west)

Choose a SEASON:
(Spring, Summer, Autumn, Winter)

What do you SEE?

What do you HEAR?

What do you SMELL?

What do you TASTE?

What do you TOUCH?

How does this image make you FEEL?

BRAINSTORM EXAMPLE

Use the following POETIC DEVICES to describe your image.
Write words, phrases, and/or full lines.

PERSONIFICATION:
(something is given humanlike characteristics)

she (sunset) drapes her warm rays across the sky,
embracing the end of the day

ALLITERATION:
(two or more words begin with the same letter/sound in a line)

sweet strawberry ice cream, squawking seagulls,
shimmering sugar white sand, sparkling sea

METAPHOR:
(two objects are compared directly, showing an unlikely similarity)

the sun is a juicy peach, ripe with want and satisfying
the sun is love blanketing the cloudy sky in a burst of color

YOUR CHOICE:

List as many COLORS as you need to describe your image:

golden, tangerine, turquoise, violet, sapphire,
emerald, sugar white, cyan, baby blue

List as many ING WORDS (Present Participles)
to describe your image:

shimmering, sparkling, laughing, spinning, playing, sizzling

BRAINSTORM

Use the following POETIC DEVICES to describe your image.
Write words, phrases, and/or full lines.

PERSONIFICATION:
(something is given humanlike characteristics)

ALLITERATION:
(two or more words begin with the same letter/sound in a line)

METAPHOR:
(two objects are compared directly, showing an unlikely similarity)

YOUR CHOICE:

List as many COLORS as you need to describe your image:

List as many ING WORDS (Present Participles)
to describe your image:

Sunset on the Beach

The *golden* sun is *love*
Blanketing the sky in a burst
of *butterscotch* and *tangerine*.

She drapes her *warm* rays
Across the sky
Extinguishing the light at the end of the joyous day--
The heat no longer *scorching* my skin

Sugar white, gritty sand *tickles* my toes
As the *shimmering* sea *laps* at them with *greedy* fingers
In a *rumbling* rhythm.

I watch silver dolphins
Spinning up out of the crisp waves
Bursting free
From the crystal blue water
And carrying my happiness in their hearts
As I drag my *wandering* mind back to reality.

Brooke E. Wayne

Sunset on the Beach

The *blistering* sun is an *angry, old man*
Smothering the sky in a burst
Of *smoky gray* and *plum.*

He wraps his *cruel, clamoring* rays
Across the sandy beach
Strangling the light at the end of the *weary* day--
The heat no longer *boiling* my skin.

Gritty, annoying sand *scruffs up* my toes
As the *hazy, azure* sea *claws* at them with *foamy* fingers
In a *thundering* rhythm.

I peer at the slippery dolphins
Spiraling up out of the icy cold waves
Breaking loose
From the glassy sea
And destroying my heartless reverie
As I drag my *lazy* mind back into reality.

Brooke E. Wayne

Sunset Over Mountains

Crisp, cold mountain air
Fills my lungs in a tight rush of excitement.
Ski slopes cry out for my attention,
Beckoning me to play one more time,
While silent, silver snowflakes drift down
in a quiet surrender
As the simmering sun
slides behind violet mountains.

Sunset Over the City

Shadowy, tall towers
Loom on the horizon, mirroring the magenta sky
The city breathes out a cacophony
Of bustling people everywhere,
Determined to find their way home
Before the vibrant persimmon sun
slips into the darkness
And calls it a night.

Brooke E. Wayne

Write

....
(title of your poem)

The .... sun is (a/an) ....
    (adjective--description)   (concrete or abstract noun--object or feeling)

.... the sky in a burst
(present participle--ING word)

of .... and ....
    (color)   (color)

She wraps her .... rays
          (present participle--ING word)

Across the ....
      (location)

Extinguishing the light at the end of the .... day--
                (adjective--description)

The heat no longer .... my skin.
       (present participle--ING word)

................................., ... sand .... my toes
(adjective--description) (adjective--description)   (verb--action)

As the .... sea .... at them with .... fingers
  (adjective--description)   (verb)   (adjective--description)

In a .... rhythm.
    (present participle--ING word)

I ....
  (synonym for "look")   (describe something in your location)

....
(describe what the object is doing)

As I drag my .... mind back to reality.
     (adjective--description)

....
(your name)

Write

_____

_____

_____

_____

_____

_____

_____

_____

_____

_____

_____

_____

_____

_____

_____

_____

_____

_____

_____

Structured Poetry

Hey? Psst. Are you easily intimidated
by being left alone with a blank sheet of paper
and nothing but your brilliant ideas?
When I find myself struggling to come up with something--
anything--to get my creative writing on
when all the words are there, they just need an outlet--
one technique I resort to is structured poetry.
This is the part where I scratch my head and think,
hmm, should I have put this section closer to the beginning?
Eh, it's too late now.
I did give you a tip to flip around earlier, though,
so there's that.
In the next section,
I highlight a handful of some of my favorite types of poems.
I've even penned a few examples for you to ooh and ahh over.
Just kidding.
(Please don't groan in pain when you read them, though, okay?)
The poetry I have written does come from my heart,
and, as you know by now,
it's a shady, loving, oddball chamber
of weird and wonderful musings.
Having said that, I'll just go slink back over here in the corner
and let you get to the next set of lessons.
Sorry not sorry.

STRUCTURED POETRY
Haiku
Tanka
Couplets &
Quatrains
Limerick
Cento

HAIKU

An ancient Japanese poem celebrating nature that consists of seventeen syllables broken into three lines.
Line One: 5 syllables
Line Two: 7 syllables
Line Three: 5 syllables

EXAMPLE:

Crisp morning sea breeze
Presses against the window
In a silent hush

EXAMPLE:

Shattered forest light
On a dark and weathered path
Soon the dawn will rise

Pluck one-liners from each list and string together some practice **HAIKU.**
You can also alter some words, just maintain the proper syllabic count per line, and celebrate nature!

5 SYLLABLE ONE-LINERS

ancient memories
glistening starlight
crisp morning sea breeze
dew drenched spiderweb
mist covered valley
bright glowing embers
shattered forest light
deep thoughts awaken

7 SYLLABLE ONE-LINERS

casting indigo shadows
awakening thoughts of day
images flash in my mind
presses against the window
stirring my calm enchantment
on a dark and weathered path
fireflies begin to glow
a meadow awaits spring buds

5 SYLLABLE ONE-LINERS

on this peaceful lake
with a joyful praise
on the journey home
promises kept true
soon the dawn will rise
in a silent hush
Autumn celebrates
nature calls my name

HAIKU might be traditionally focused on nature, but, as a poet, you can add your personal touch to its unique, rhythmical structure. Write original Haiku celebrating all kinds of events, emotions, or experiences. The choice is yours! Here are some examples of alternate-themed Haiku poems:

CLASSIC HAIKU

Winter solitude–
In a world of one colour
The sound of the wind

Matsuo Bashō

Spring morning marvel
Lovely nameless little hill,
On a sea of mist

Matsuo Bashō

April's air stirs in
Willow leaves ... a butterfly
Floats and balances

Matsuo Bashō

Matsuo Bashō (1644-1694)
is regarded as the master
of Japanese poetry
during the Edo period in Japan.
He studied haikai no renga
which is a collaborative
composition of several verses.
The opening of a renga
(known as a hokku)
is the foundation of what
has eventually become known
as the Haiku because of its
three unrhyming lines
made up of a
5, 7, 5 syllabic pattern.

MODERN HAIKU

In one fleeting glance
I saw your heart and you mine
Entangled in fate

Robin Woods

You think I am trapped
I smile tightly in hate
Knowing I will leave

Robin Woods

Conquering my fears
My destiny is my own,
I rise up with grace

Robin Woods

Make the world better
One small kindness at a time
Start with a smile

Robin Woods

Sleepless nights, Your face
imprinted deep on my lids
entrancing my soul

Robin Woods

A special thanks to author
and friend, Robin Woods, for
sharing her Haiku.

MODERN HAIKU

Enchanted lovesong
Curling around our hearts
Silenced by Love's hum

Brooke E. Wayne

"Come on in students.
Blah, blah, blah, blah, blah, blah, blah.
See you tomorrow."

Brooke E. Wayne

Time does not heal wounds
So deep and so sorrowful
when death comes too soon

Brooke E. Wayne

Imagination
Set me free from the boredom
I need to escape

Brooke E. Wayne

Check out more Haiku
poetry from yours truly.
Simply click on the
QR Code to be redirected
to all that sllyabic awesomeness.

WRITE

_____

_____

_____

_____

_____

_____

_____

_____

_____

_____

_____

_____

_____

_____

_____

_____

_____

_____

_____

WRITE

TANKA

An ancient Japanese poem that consists of thirty-one syllables broken into seven lines.
Line One: 5 syllables
Line Two: 7 syllables
Line Three: 5 syllables
Line Four: 7 syllables
Line Five: 7 syllables

Unlike Haiku where nature
takes center stage,
the Tanka focuses
on a single subject
that has no restrictions.
The last two lines
of the poem; however,
illicit an emotional response
to the subject being celebrated.

Grab one-liners from each list and fashion together some practice Tanka.
You can also alter some words, just maintain the proper syllabic count per line, and celebrate a compelling subject!

5 SYLLABLE ONE-LINERS

timeless wonderings
shimmering river
waiting endlessly
magnificent sun
holding your soft hand
cherishing our time
a sweet surrender
I hold onto you
adrift on the sea
secrets buried deep
with his hand in mine
with her heart in mine
promises are kept
like a raging storm

7 SYLLABLE ONE-LINERS

cherishing my time with you
stirring thoughts of yester-year
my heart beats only for you
with your love deep in my heart
quiet moments all alone
the world seems so far away
endless stars that shine so bright
a choreographed lovesong
a meadow of endless blue
in my quiet solitude
giving into your embrace
looking at me in true love
above us--a cityscape
in a moment of weakness

ADMIRER

Secrets buried deep
Within my heart in stillness
Waiting endlessly
To capture a glimpse of you
Looking back at me in love

Brooke E. Wayne

INTIMACY

A sweet surrender
Giving into your embrace
My heart--full of love
And my soul full of yearning
I am home within your arms

Brooke E. Wayne

TRANQUILITY

Magnificent moon
Bathing me in pale, cool light
Stars are shimmering
A choreographed lovesong
As I exhale all my stress

Brooke E. Wayne

Tanka poetry typically doesn't have titles.
I may have taken some rebellious liberties
in putting titles on these charmers.
If you haven't zapped the QR code on the
Haiku page and gandered at all my
examples, then what are you waiting for?
So much title eye candy! I'm a big doer of
punchline titles with all my books, too.
It's how I roll. Carry on.

WRITE

WRITE

_____

_____

_____

_____

_____

_____

_____

_____

_____

_____

_____

_____

_____

_____

_____

_____

_____

COUPLETS & QUATRAINS

A couplet is a two-line stanza. The last word of each line rhymes together.

A quatrain is a four-line stanza with an alternating rhyme scheme of ABAB.
Alternately: ABAC, ABCB, ABBA, AABA

RHYMING WORDS:

true, hue, anew, renew, through
wonder, thunder, blunder,
yearning, learning, burning
love, glove, shove, above, of
strong, song, belong, long, along
broken, token, oaken, spoken
sweet, street, cheat, concrete, seat
rain, brain, chain, slain, stain, lane
afinity, divinity, infinity, femininity
trinity, masculinity, proximity
emotion, ocean, devotion, notion
cherish, garish, perish
prayed, cascade, blade, crusade
day, play, say, away, pray, stay
enchant, decadent, plant, rant
tears, fears, appears, years, cheers

SUFFIXES TO GENERATE RHYMES

--ist
--ion
--tion
--sion
--ed
--er
--or
--ful
--less
--ness
--ly
--ship
--ence
--ance
--ace
--ite
--ible
--able
--ment
--ant
--ent

RYHMING WORDS RESOURCES:

www.rhymezone.com
www.rhymes.net
www.rhymedb.com
www.wikirhymer.com

Invent some couplets with the examples,
and alternate the lines to create the classic
rhyme scheme of ABAB.
Create a list of words that wow you,
and plug them into the rhyme generators
on the websites above to create your own sets.

COUPLETS & QUATRAINS EXAMPLES

The Table in the Wilderness

Between the lines of time and space,
All who gather dine in saving grace.

And everyone arrives ready to be strong,
Because this is where they know they belong.

No longer does anyone feel weary and broken,
As they fellowship together with words unspoken--

At the table in the wilderness.

Brooke E. Wayne

RIP BWC
(Poem Composed of Couplets: AABBCCD)

Thirteen Years and Staying Strong

Just look into my eyes, and you'll know how I feel;
This love I carry in my heart is all too real.
Romance aside, there's a passion to our love,
Like we're destined for each other, orchestrated from Above.

Brooke E. Wayne

JAM--I love you.
(Quatrain: AABB)

Guess what? I not a fan of writing poems that rhyme. I'm Free Verse all the way. This might be your strength, though. If you love writing poems that rhyme, consider your ability to write using a Rhyme Scheme your super power. You rock!

WRITE

WRITE

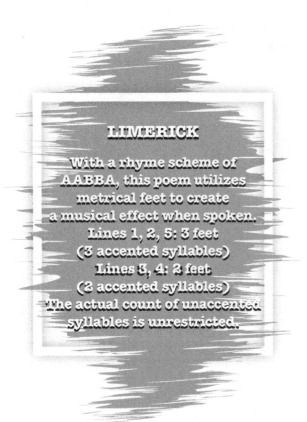

LIMERICK

With a rhyme scheme of AABBA, this poem utilizes metrical feet to create a musical effect when spoken.
Lines 1, 2, 5: 3 feet
(3 accented syllables)
Lines 3, 4: 2 feet
(2 accented syllables)
The actual count of unaccented syllables is unrestricted.

RYHMING WORDS RESOURCES:

www.rhymezone.com
www.rhymes.net
www.rhymedb.com
www.wikirhymer.com

Be honest. You totally skimmed through all the instructional pages in the beginning of this workbook, didn't you? You're thinking s$#%! I don't know what the heck meters and feet have to do with writing. So now what do I do? Here's a recap for you because I'm nice like that.

FEET: groups of syllables (not words—could be one word or several) making up a string of syllables both accented (hard sound) and unaccented (soft sound).

METER: The rhythm or beat created by the number of stressed/unstressed accents present in the feet.

I get that mathematics can be horrific--counting all those accented syllables within a metric foot inside a verse. Sheesh!
It scares me, too.
Not to mention the anxiety in just finding the right words to express yourself in your poem.
No wonder this type of poem pairs well with Guinness!
(Ignore that if you're a teen!)
Hear me out, though.
There's a down and dirty way to learn how to write a Limerick without all the stress of counting stressed syllables.
Ready for it?

PRO TIP:
All you have to do is look up some Limericks online, and read them out loud.
Three or four Limericks deep, and you'll be dipping your head, tapping your foot, and feeling the rhythm in your bones.

Here is one basic accented pattern.
Remember, 'da' unaccented syllables are not set, just the accented ones--the 'dum' ones, you know?

Da-**dum**, da-da-**dum**, da-da-**dum**
Da-**dum**, da-da-**dum**, da-da-**dum**
Da-**dum**, da-da-**dum**,
Da-**dum**, da-da-**dum**
Da-**dum**, da-da-**dum**, da-da-**dum**

Composing a **LIMERICK** can feel daunting. The quickest way to start is to decide on three words for the A lines in the rhyme scheme. Then decide on the hook for your first verse. I went with the classic **There once was a...** for my example. Toy around with the subject matter until something humorous or pithy emerges. Keep it clean, like me, or go naughty–maybe even pour a pint, if you're an adult, to set a saucy mood for some ye' ol' dry humor. The short B verses will click because of the sing-songy meter.

LIMERICK
#1

There once was a poet with a crush.
She pined day and night writing mush.
The words were absurd,
But none he had heard,
Since those silly poems made even her blush!

Brooke E. Wayne

Dig deep and find that one thing that cracks you up no matter how goofy or crude it is. Then, come up with a set of three rhyming words and a set of two rhyming words--keeping them as simple as possible for flexibility with the verses! As you play around with the story, try to work your way towards those rhyming words. You'll have Limericks mastered in no time!

WRITE

_____

_____

_____

_____

_____

_____

_____

_____

_____

_____

_____

_____

_____

_____

_____

_____

_____

WRITE

_____

_____

_____

_____

_____

_____

_____

_____

_____

_____

_____

_____

_____

_____

_____

_____

_____

_____

CENTO ("Patchwork")

A Cento poem borrows singular lines from famous poems, knitting together an original poem. Traditionally, each line must come from a different poet.

Tweak the classic take on a CENTO and create a unique poem that expresses your feelings and thoughts by stringing together one-liners from your favorite ...

SONG TITLES
SONG LYRICS
OPENING LINES OF NOVELS
LAST LINES OF NOVELS
QUOTES FROM NOVELS
PRODUCT SLOGANS
MULTICULTURAL PROVERBS

You can also ...

MAKE A CENTO COMPOSED OF LINES THAT FIT INTO A PARTICULAR RHYME SCHEME

FAMOUS POETS of the PAST:

Walt Whitman
Robert Frost
William Shakespeare
Emily Dickinson
Emily Brontë
Charlotte Brontë
Anne Brontë
Edgar Allan Poe
Ernest Hemmingway
Hoxuan Huong
Jane Austen
J. R. R. Tolkien
Ambrose Bierce
Henry David Thoreau
Langston Hughes
John Keats
Percy Bysshe Shelley
James Joyce
Ralph Waldo Emerson
Alfred Lord Tennyson
Henry Wadsworth Longfellow
Dylan Thomas
Robert Browning
Elizabeth Barrett Browning
Robert Burns
Rupert Brooke
William Butler Yeats
Rudyard Kipling
Dorothy Parker
Oscar Wilde
William Carlos Williams
Matsuo Basho
John Donne
Victor Hugo
Sylvia Plath
William Wordsworth
Clement Clarke Moore
Robert Louis Stevenson
e. e. cummings

MORE RECENT POETS:

Maya Angelou
Shel Silverstein
Roald Dahl

Everything Carries Me to You

You are violets with wind above them
    And shreds of shadowy laughter
        That looks on tempests and is never shaken.
One kind glance from thine eye,
    In which the Heart is caught,
        And I'll forget the past!
For One must wait
    To find if hearts be wild and wise ...
So long as the world contains us both,
    Love's web is spun.

Brooke E. Wayne

Attributes:
(Title--Pablo Neruda, "If You Forget Me")
(Line 1--Ezra Pound, "A Girl")
(Line 2--Rupert Brooke, "Beauty and Beauty")
(Line 3--William Shakespeare, "Sonnet 116")
(Line 4--Charlotte Brontë, "Passion")
(Line 5--Emily Dickinson, "Escape is such a thankful Word")
(Line 6--Jane Austen, "Oh! Mr. Best You're Very Bad")
(Line 7--Emily Dickinson, "I cannot live with You")
(Line 8--William Butler Yeats, "The Mask")
(Line 9--Robert Browning, "Life in a Love")
(Line 10--Oscar Wilde, "Her Voice")

WRITE

Prompts

Hey? Psst. For some writers, a literal tabula rasa (blank slate)
is their ultimate go-to for writing of all kinds of awesomeness.
Hand 'em a sheet of paper or a New Document,
and their eyes glaze over, then away they go,
making words like nobody's business.
I'm like that about, hmm, 75% of the time.
Other writers don't operate that way.
They're clinching their fists and wallowing in writer's block
--oh, no wait, that's me the other 25% of the time--
other writers are probably hunting down inspiration
to ignite their writerly passion.
What inspires can come in all kinds of flavors.
Sometimes a nudge, like one of my off-the-wall prompts,
can give the whirlwind of creativity breath
to those writers who need a pathway to get writing.
I tried to cultivate a broad range of concepts,
but feel free to tweak any of the prompts to suit your taste.
Don't forget to stuff those babies full of poetic devices,
and swap out any of my suggestions, if it pleases.
I'll be over here cheering you on
and brainstorming my next grouping of prompts
for a Volume 2 workbook.
Say, what?!

WONDROUS WORDS

ABHOR-----Feelings of disgust
AGHAST-----Filled with horror
BETROTHED-----The person one's engaged to
BEMOAN-----Expressing sorrow
CANTANKEROUS-----Argumentative and ill-tempered
CURMUDGEON-----A grumpy, old man
CONNIVE-----Play ignorant to or allow an awful event to occur
DREARY-----Lifeless or depressing, dull
ENIGMA-----Puzzling thing or mysterious person
FERVOR-----An intense emotional expression
GAUNT-----So thin one appears malnourished
HYSTERICAL-----Uncontrollable emotion
INEPT-----Incompetent or incapable
INNOCUOUS-----Harmless or ineffective
JADED-----Feeling bored after an overindulgence
KERFUFFLE-----A commotion brought on by a dispute
LAMENT-----To wail in mourning
LISTLESS-----Lacking energy or vigor
MALIGNANT-----Infectious or diseased
NEPOTISM-----Playing favorites because of kinship
OMNISCIENT-----Possessing universal knowledge
PECULIAR-----Distinct to a singular item, person, or group
QUAINT-----Old-fashioned, elegant, or odd
ROBUST-----Strong or sturdy
SHREWD-----Sharp or clever discernment
SINISTER-----Producing evil or ill will
STAGNANT-----Not advancing, or flowing
TUMULTUOUS-----Aggressive turbulence or upheaval
TENACIOUS-----Cleaving or clinging to, adhering to
UBIQUITOUS-----Existing everywhere
VEHEMENT-----Bitterly impassioned
WIZENED-----Shriveled up and dried by age
YIELDING-----Productive or flexible

PROMPT #1

We all live in a world
of our own,
coexisting in the present
with our unique points-of-view
interpreting,
manipulating,
and experiencing
our version of this life
as we wish.

In a free verse narrative,
write about a
DAY
IN THE LIFE
OF YOU.

WRITE

PROMPT #2

Go outside tonight
and
LOOK UP.

What do you see?
... a sliver of moon?
... a blanket of stars?
... nothing but clouded darkness?

How do you feel?
Can you connect this moment
to an experience
in your life
as a metaphor?

WRITE

_____

_____

_____

_____

_____

_____

_____

_____

_____

_____

_____

_____

_____

_____

_____

_____

PROMPT #3

LUCID DREAMING
with eyes closed, mind wide open
--when reality bends
and our slumbering imaginations
drag us on a journey
we have power to control.

Would your vivd dream
change the world,
change the world inside of you,
or change
someone else's very existence?

Make this one rhyme.

Rhyme Scheme:
aabb ccdd eeff gghh iijj kkll

WRITE

_____

_____

_____

_____

_____

_____

_____

_____

_____

_____

_____

_____

_____

_____

_____

_____

_____

_____

_____

_____

PROMPT #4

Hope is a standard emotion
in writing metaphorical expressions,
an anchor tethered to our souls,
keeping us from going adrift
into the dreaded bore
of mundane despair.

Give someone
HOPE
through a metaphor
you haven't stumbled upon, yet.
Wrap your shiny, new line
in a poem
that inspires
an entirely different emotion.

WRITE

_____

_____

_____

_____

_____

_____

_____

_____

_____

_____

_____

_____

_____

_____

_____

_____

_____

_____

_____

WONDROUS WORDS

ABSCOND-----Vanish
BECOMING-----Attractive
BEGUILING-----Deceiving
CASCADE-----Overflow
DEMURE-----Shy
DESULTORY-----Half-hearted
ENCHANTING-----Charming
ENDEAVOR-----Strive
EPIPHANY-----Revelation
EVANESCENT-----Fleeting
FELICITY-----Joyfulness
GLAMOROUS-----Alluring
HARMONIOUS-----Agreeable
INCANDESCENT-----Radiant
JUBILANT-----Excited
KEEN-----Enthusiastic
LANGUID-----Listless
LOQUACIOUS-----Chatty
MELLIFLUOUS-----Smooth
NEFARIOUS-----Wicked
NIRVANA-----Bliss
OPULENT-----Luxurious
PLETHORA-----Abundance
QUIESCENT-----Slumbering
RESPLENDENT-----Blazing
SERENDIPITOUS-----Fortuitous
TRANQUILITY-----Peacefulness
UNIQUE-----Special
VESTIGE-----Remnant
WONDROUS-----Inspiring
XERIC-----Arid
YEARNING-----Longing
ZEPHYR-----Breeze

PROMPT #5

There's a **STRANGER** at the door.

Is it your front door?
The door to your car?
Your heart?

Who is this person
intruding on your life
unexpectantly?

Will you let the stranger in?

Fill your poem with emotions.
Then layer it with imagery.

WRITE

_____

_____

_____

_____

_____

_____

_____

_____

_____

_____

_____

_____

_____

_____

_____

_____

_____

_____

PROMPT #6

OPINIONS
matter in this world.
They elevate us,
aggravate us,
help us hone in on who we are
and what we believe,
and even get us in trouble.

Choose a controversial topic,
and write from
your least favored perspective.

Will your poem resonate
with passion or apathy?

Be sure to write it in
first person point-of-view.

WRITE

_____

_____

_____

_____

_____

_____

_____

_____

_____

_____

_____

_____

_____

_____

_____

_____

PROMPT #7

What strikes FEAR in you?
I am as creeped out by clowns
as I am having to talk to a stranger
on the phone.

If I were to articulate my feelings
about either in a poem,
I would use lots of
hyperbolic statements,
and maybe an exclamation point
or two ... or ten.

How would your fear
manifest in a poem?

WRITE

PROMPT #8

RHYME SCHEME
is a hard line rule imposed on a poem.
Choosing words
that enhance the poem's meaning
verses degrading it for the sake
of a sing-song rhythm
of a pattern is tough.

Write a FREE VERSE poem.
Choose any topic you fancy.
Then rewrite it
as closely to the original as you can
with a rhyme scheme.

Here's one:
ABBA CDDC EFFE GHHG II JJ

WRITE

WONDROUS WORDS

APPARITION-----A ghost
ASCENT-----The act of moving upward
BALDERDASH-----Nonsense
BAZAAR-----A fair or open market
BLUFF-----A steep cliff
BRAGGART-----Someone who boasts
BROUHAHA--An uproar
COLLYWOBBLES-----Butterfly sensation in the stomach
DIVERSITY-----Various kinds
DEMESNE-----Territory
DYNASTY-----Generational rulers from the same family
ELIXIR-----A good potion
EXPERTISE-----Specialized in knowledge or skill
FRISSON-----An intense moment of excitement
INSTANCE-----An example
KEN-----A range of what someone can understand
KINDRED-----A person's relatives
FACADE-----A false appearance
FIASCO-----A huge failure
FRAUDULENCE-----Deceitfulness
MISANTHROPE-----Someone who detests people in general
PARADIGM-----A typical example
PESTILENCE-----Plague
PLAIT-----A braid
PLUME-----A feather
PREMONITION-----Forewarning
RELUCTANCY-----Unable to make a decision
SAGE-----An intellectual or wise person
SEER-----A prophet
SOLIDARITY-----Unity of purpose
STOOP-----A small porch

PROMPT #9

Do you have any
SCARS
on your body?

Tell its story
through a **LIMERICK.**
(See Table of Contents: Limerick
for detailed instructions.)

Laugh through the physical
(and/or emotional) pain
it may have caused you.

Is is true when they say
laughter heals?

WRITE

_____

_____

_____

_____

_____

_____

_____

_____

_____

_____

_____

_____

_____

_____

_____

_____

_____

PROMPT #10

THREE WISHES
stories use a wonderful,
albeit cliché, trope.

Turn the concept
of three wishes
into a three-stanza poem
with a rhyme scheme.

Rewrite it
as a free verse poem,
and turn one of the wishes
into a humorous catastrophy.

WRITE

_____

_____

_____

_____

_____

_____

_____

_____

_____

_____

_____

_____

_____

_____

_____

_____

_____

PROMPT #11

If you could
TRAVEL IN TIME,
who would you approach,
and what would you say?

Would you seek out
your younger self,
someone who has passed away,
or an old friend
you've lost touch with?

Fill the encounter with emotions,
and bring the time period to life
with imagery.

WRITE

_____

_____

_____

_____

_____

_____

_____

_____

_____

_____

_____

_____

_____

_____

_____

_____

_____

PROMPT #12

Choose one word to
INSPIRE
and unleash your imagination.

Pick from the list.
Choose them all.
Choose one.
Or come up with your own word.

Flood your poem
with alliteration and imagery.

wander, family, spirit, light, weep,
school, kindness, dessert, escape,
shallow, dark matter, team,
heaven, country, hero, talent,
friendship, nightmare, leaves,
book, talent, sky, colors, cheese

WRITE

WONDROUS WORDS

AMAZING-----Astonishing, Fantastic, Wonderful
AVERAGE-----Customary, Standard, Traditional
BIG-----Enormous, Grand, Humongous
COLD-----Chilled, Frigid, Frosty
COME-----Approach, Arrive, Reach
DARK-----Dismal, Gloomy, Shadowy
DECIDE-----Commit, Determine, Resolve
END-----Cease, Conclude, Dissolve
FAKE-----Deceptive, Erroneous, Fraudulent
ENOUGH-----Adequate, Ample, Satisfactory
GO-----Journey, Proceed, Travel
GREAT-----Glorious, Spectacular, Splendid
HAVE-----Maintain, Obtain, Possess
HOLD-----Embrace, Grasp, Grip
HOT-----Torrid, Scorching, Smoldering
LIKE-----Enjoy, Devour, Savor
MAKE-----Create, Manifest, Produce
KNOWN-----Celebrated, Noteworthy, Renowned
LOOK-----Gaze, Glare, Glance
MOVE-----Dawdle, Meander, Promenade
NEW-----Fresh, Modern, Unique
ODD-----Eccentric, Peculiar, Unique
RUIN-----Destroy, Fracture, Shatter
RUN-----Gallop, Trot, Sprint
SAY-----Whisper, Shout, Bark
SEE-----Behold, Gaze, Stare, Gawk
SHOW-----Display, Exibit, Present
SLOW-----Gradual, Leisurely, Tedious
SPEAK-----Converse, Declare, Pronounce
STAND-----Slouch, Poise, Perch
START-----Begin, Commence, Initiate
TAKE-----Capture, Clutch, Snatch
TOUCH-----Caress, Grasp, Embrace
WALK-----Amble, Prance, Stride

PROMPT #13

We've all read that one book
or short story that thrills us,
tapping into our imagination
and giving us a big ol' sigh
when we'd consumed that final word
--or maybe that's just me.

Confession: I read a lot of
Romantic Comedies,
and I write them, too.
I relish in meet-cutes
and happily-ever-afters.
Perhaps, you're a fan
of sci-fi or horror,
but, instead of sighing, you scream.

Nevertheless,
recall something you've read
that left an **IMPRESSION** on you.
Now, condense and transform the plot
into a one-page poem
littered with similes and metaphors
about how the story made you feel.

WRITE

_____

_____

_____

_____

_____

_____

_____

_____

_____

_____

_____

_____

_____

_____

_____

_____

_____

_____

PROMPT #14

Take a journey
on foot, in a car, on a train, on a bus,
in an airplane--
oh, the Dr. Seuss feels abound!

Joking aside,
write about the
THRESHOLD
of the journey.

Use personification
with the vehicle
during the rush of departure,
and use a hyperbole to describe
that first space you fill
that takes you out of your comfort zone
and onto an unchartered path
where adventure awaits
farther away.

WRITE

_____

_____

_____

_____

_____

_____

_____

_____

_____

_____

_____

_____

_____

_____

_____

_____

_____

PROMPT #15

We're all familiar
with the proverial hallway
of endless doors to choose from--
life's metaphorical choices.

Instead of writing
about the adventure
behind a chosen door,
craft a poem
that describes the
APPEARANCE OF EACH DOOR
beckoning the traveler.
Which door will your reader
want to choose?
What kind of quest
does is appear to harbor?
What could possibly
go wrong?

WRITE

_____

_____

_____

_____

_____

_____

_____

_____

_____

_____

_____

_____

_____

_____

_____

_____

_____

_____

PROMPT #16

Listen to an entire music album
by one of your favorite artists.
The collection should tell a story
or make an overall statement.

Write another
SONG
to add to the album
that captures its message.

Incorporate repetition as a chorus,
and try to match the rhyme scheme
evident in at least one
of the album's original songs.
Don't forget to pack it full
of strong emotions!

WRITE

WONDROUS WORDS

ABSQUATULATE-----Abruptly leave

BANE-----Poison

BETOKEN-----A warning

BILLOW-----A huge ocean wave

BOOTLESS-----Of no use

CACOETHES-----Desire to do something reckless

CANOROUS-----Resonant

DEASIL-----Clockwise

DEGUST-----To slowly savor food or drink for pleasure

DIVAGATE-----To stray

EFFABLE-----Able to use words to describe

ERUBESCENT-----Blushing or reddening

GALLANT-----Gentleman-like conduct

GLAIVE-----A sword

HAUGHTY-----Proud

HINKY-----Suspicious, dishonest

INEFFABLE-----Too grand to be expressed with words

KNELL-----A bell's resonance

LUCULENT-----Precisely expressed in writing or spoken

MANIFOLD-----Various

NESCIENT-----Ignorant or unknowing

ORGULOUS-----Haughty

PERFERVID-----Impassioned

PLIGHT-----A promise or pledge

REFULGENT-----Radiant

SANS-----Without

SYLVAN-----Wooded

TEMERARIOUS-----Reckless or irrational

TENEBROUS-----Dark and shadowy

TRAVAIL-----Exhaustive effort

UMBRIFEROUS-----Shady

WHENCE-----Where something has come from

YORE-----Long ago

PROMPT #17

Make
INNER STRENGTH
the focus of your poem.

Whether it is abounding or lacking,
include the drive to go forth
and keep moving forward.

What motivates you
to stay strong?

Include a few onomatopoeia
to enhance the energy
of the poem.
Try to personify strength, too.

WRITE

_____

_____

_____

_____

_____

_____

_____

_____

_____

_____

_____

_____

_____

_____

_____

_____

_____

PROMPT #18

A dash of this,
a smidgen of that--
sprinkle a little bit of
imagery on top
with a side of
similes and metaphors
to describe youself
if you were a
MEAL.

Like a sweet rice crispy treat--
all those individual,
puffed-up rice smothered
in marshmallow cream,
I'm all about my family
sticking together.

Would your poem
feed someone's hungry soul?

WRITE

_____

_____

_____

_____

_____

_____

_____

_____

_____

_____

_____

_____

_____

_____

_____

_____

PROMPT #19

PROVERBS
are those cultural expressions
that speak of
wisdom and truth.
Create a list of your own proverbs
that resonate with your
personal values.

Can you transform some of them
into implied metaphors?

Write your proverbs in the form of
Haiku.
(See Table of Contents: Haiku
for directions.)

WRITE

_____
_____
_____
_____
_____
_____
_____
_____
_____
_____
_____
_____
_____
_____
_____
_____
_____

PROMPT #20

Not gonna lie.
I loathe acrostic poems.
You remember those, don't you?
Harken back to elementary school
when you listed adjectives
behind each letter of your name
that started with the same letter
and described you.
Wouldn't it be fun to write an
ACROSTIC POEM
about something you hated?
Load that miserable excuse
of creativity
with all the bad words
and, don't forget,
alliterative ones, too.

WRITE

WONDROUS WORDS

ABSTAIN-----To choose to avoid something

AFFIRM-----To declare or assert

APPEASE-----To pacify or calm down

APPRISE-----To inform

BELITTLE-----To bully with disrespectful words

BESIEGE-----To harass or plead with offerings

BESTOW-----To honor, grant, or present a gift to someone

BRAG-----To tell everyone about one's greatness or accomplishments

COLLABORATE-----To work cooperatively

CULMINATE-----To conclude or reach the highest degree

DISCOMFIT-----To frustrate

DISPARAGE-----To speak of in a belittling manner

DISTORT-----To misrepresent or to twist askew

EMERGE-----To rise out of something

ENDORSE-----To recommend someone or something

EXPEND-----To consume or use up

INFURIATE-----To enrage with anger

NECESSITATE-----To justify as useful or required

OBLITERATE-----To demolish

PERSEVERE-----To strive towards a goal regardless of struggles

PLACATE-----To calm down or appease

PULVERIZE-----To crush into powder

RATIFY-----To cofirm, give sanction to, or approve

REFURBISH-----To renovate or renew

REINFORCE-----To strengthen or increase in volume

REFUTE-----To disapprove or prove false

SYNCOPATE-----To shorten by dropping sounds or letters or to modify rhythm

UNIFY-----To come together as one

VANQUISH-----To conquer or overcome

VERIFY-----To prove to be accurate

VILIFY-----To regard something in a disparaging manner

PROMPT #21

Have you ever desired something
so much it ached?

That **LONGING** for something
just out of reach
has you clamoring towards it,
and nothing can stop you
until it is yours.
The emotional charge is an
eclectic,
piercing,
hope-driven hunger,
and your poem should capture
the passion of your pursuit.

Add some hyperbole
to illustrate that
over-the-top ambition
you have to reach that goal.

WRITE

_____

_____

_____

_____

_____

_____

_____

_____

_____

_____

_____

_____

_____

_____

_____

_____

_____

_____

PROMPT #22

When the general population
thinks of romance,
imaginings of hearts and flowers
tend to pop in their heads.
Romance and poetry go hand in hand.
Think of someone you've had
romantic feelings for
like a boyfriend, girlfriend,
spouse, or even a celebrity crush.
Capture those feelings in a
TANKA
(See Table of Contents: Tanka
for instructions.)

Does this person know
you feel or felt this way?

Was that romantic feeling
true love?

WRITE

PROMPT #23

The first and last line of a novel
must always be impactful.
They hook the reader,
usually with a poetic device
like imagery.
The last lines of a work
always gives the reader
a sense of closure.
Using the first and last lines
from your favorite
novels,
short stories,
and poems,
compile a patchword-style
CENTO
of those one-liners
to create an original poem
that reflects the type of
writing you like to read.

WRITE

_____

_____

_____

_____

_____

_____

_____

_____

_____

_____

_____

_____

_____

_____

_____

_____

_____

PROMPT #24

Reread one of your favorite poems.
Did you write it or did someone else?
What poetic devices were used
to create such a compelling poem?

Try to rewrite a
POEM,
changing up the poetic devices
to different ones.

Does it change the tone of the poem?
What mood does it create
for the reader?

Whether it's one of your poems
or someone else's,
did it make the poem
better or worse?

WRITE

_____

_____

_____

_____

_____

_____

_____

_____

_____

_____

_____

_____

_____

_____

_____

_____

_____

_____

WONDROUS WORDS

ADROIT-----Skillful, deft, and dexterous
AMIABLE-----Friendly or pleasant
AMPLE-----Abundant or substantial
BELLIGERENT-----Hostile or aggressive
CALAMITOUS-----Catastrophic or disastrous
CAPACIOUS-----Able to contain a large quantity, spacious
CELESTIAL-----Pertaining to the heavens
CYNICAL-----Sarcastic or distrusting in others' values
DESPONDENT-----Feeling drepressed or disheartened
EMINENT-----Famous or well-known
EXORBITANT-----Extravagant or excessive
EXTRAVAGANT-----Extremely abundant or lavish
FACETIOUS-----Flippant about a serious matter
FALLIBLE-----Capable of making mistakes
FORMIDABLE-----Provoking fear due to size, strength or power
GENIAL-----Kind and friendly
GULLIBLE-----Easily deceived
HAPHAZARD-----Random or without a pattern
IRREFUTABLE-----Undeniable or incontestable
ILLOGICAL-----Irrational or confusing
INSIGNIFICANT-----Weak or powerless
LATENT-----Potential or possible
NOTORIOUS-----Well-known and disapproving
OUTLANDISH-----Strange in manner or appearance
PLAUSIBLE-----Believable and acceptable
PROMINENT-----Distinguished or notable
RECIPROCAL-----Mutual or having a likeminded attitude
THRIFTY-----Modest, cheap, or restrained
TROUBLESOME-----Causing inconvenience
ULTIMATE-----Supreme or eventual
UPROARIOUS-----Boisterous or unrestrained

PROMPT #25

COMFORT
can be a simple pleasure.
Be it a pair of pajamas,
a pile of spaghetti,
or a warm cup of herbal tea.
Comforts can nourish the soul.

What comforts you?
Write a poem
about an object
that brings you peace.
Use several
similes or metaphors
that reveal
your emotional connection
to that physical thing.

WRITE

PROMPT #26

We've all made mistakes.
Living with regret is a natural part
of being human.
We learn from our choices--
good or bad, but, what if
we could change
a choice we have made?

How would your life be different
if fate handed you a do-over?
What events would transpire
or crumble
under the power of your
CHOICE?

Write a limerick poem
making light of your mistake,
and change your fate
with your alternate ending
as the punchline.

WRITE

_____

_____

_____

_____

_____

_____

_____

_____

_____

_____

_____

_____

_____

_____

_____

_____

_____

_____

PROMPT #27

What sets your heart on fire?
Those who truly know you
know this is what defines you.
If you don't know,
then do you know someone
whose **PASSION** is so apparent,
you're drawn to them because of it.
My passion is creative writing.
What is yours (or theirs)?

Write a poem with six quatrains.
For each stanza,
answer the questions:

Who?
What?
When?
Where?
How?
Why?

WRITE

_____

_____

_____

_____

_____

_____

_____

_____

_____

_____

_____

_____

_____

_____

_____

_____

_____

PROMPT #28

WOULD YOU RATHER
be an eagle soaring above the storm
or a shark looming fearless
in the deep blue sea?

Are you most alive
in the sky,
on land,
or under the sea?
Mountains or country?
Do you reign or cower?

Write a metaphorical poem
as if you are any other creature
than a human being.
Describe your
geographical location
and how you engage
with your environment.

WRITE

WRITE

Pictorial Inspiration

Hey? Psst. I just want you to know,
before you head into the final exercise,
I've enjoyed every step of this journey alongside you.
Funny how poetry can bring out the emotions in somebody
--strangers even--only I hope that you feel a kinship with me
now that we're almost done. Or are we?
I've had such an awe-inspiring time
writing this workbook for you, daydreaming as I go
about the magnificent poetry you've written
and the wondrous person you are
behind all those exciting words.
I'm even brainstorming another
<u>Come Write with Me</u> workbook because of my,
hmm, my imagination, I guess.
It's gotten me all misty thinking
something brilliant has just happened.
I'm hoping to hear from you ...
maybe even use some of your poetry as examples
in my next project. Time will tell.
If words were musical notes,
I think we all just created
a symphonic masterpiece, don't you?
Until next time ...
~Brooke E. Wayne

PHOTO PROMPT #1

Brainstorming:

_____

_____

_____

_____

_____

_____

_____

_____

_____

_____

WRITE

_____

_____

_____

_____

_____

_____

_____

_____

_____

_____

_____

_____

_____

_____

_____

_____

_____

_____

_____

PHOTO PROMPT #2

Brainstorming:

_____

_____

_____

_____

_____

_____

_____

_____

_____

WRITE

_____

_____

_____

_____

_____

_____

_____

_____

_____

_____

_____

_____

_____

_____

_____

_____

_____

_____

PHOTO PROMPT #3

Brainstorming:

_____

_____

_____

_____

_____

_____

_____

_____

_____

_____

WRITE

_____

_____

_____

_____

_____

_____

_____

_____

_____

_____

_____

_____

_____

_____

_____

_____

_____

PHOTO PROMPT #4

Brainstorming:

_____

_____

_____

_____

_____

_____

_____

_____

_____

_____

WRITE

_____

_____

_____

_____

_____

_____

_____

_____

_____

_____

_____

_____

_____

_____

_____

_____

_____

PHOTO PROMPT #5

Brainstorming:

_____

_____

_____

_____

_____

_____

_____

_____

_____

_____

WRITE

_____

_____

_____

_____

_____

_____

_____

_____

_____

_____

_____

_____

_____

_____

_____

_____

_____

_____

PHOTO PROMPT #6

Brainstorming:

_____

_____

_____

_____

_____

_____

_____

_____

_____

PHOTO PROMPT #7

Brainstorming:

_____

_____

_____

_____

_____

_____

_____

_____

_____

_____

_____

WRITE

_____

_____

_____

_____

_____

_____

_____

_____

_____

_____

_____

_____

_____

_____

_____

_____

_____

_____

PHOTO PROMPT #8

Brainstorming:

_____

_____

_____

_____

_____

_____

_____

_____

_____

_____

_____

WRITE

_____

_____

_____

_____

_____

_____

_____

_____

_____

_____

_____

_____

_____

_____

_____

_____

_____

_____

PHOTO PROMPT #9

Brainstorming:

_____

_____

_____

_____

_____

_____

_____

_____

_____

_____

WRITE

_____

_____

_____

_____

_____

_____

_____

_____

_____

_____

_____

_____

_____

_____

_____

_____

_____

_____

PHOTO PROMPT #10

Brainstorming:

_____
_____
_____
_____
_____
_____
_____
_____
_____
_____

WRITE

_____

_____

_____

_____

_____

_____

_____

_____

_____

_____

_____

_____

_____

_____

_____

_____

_____

_____

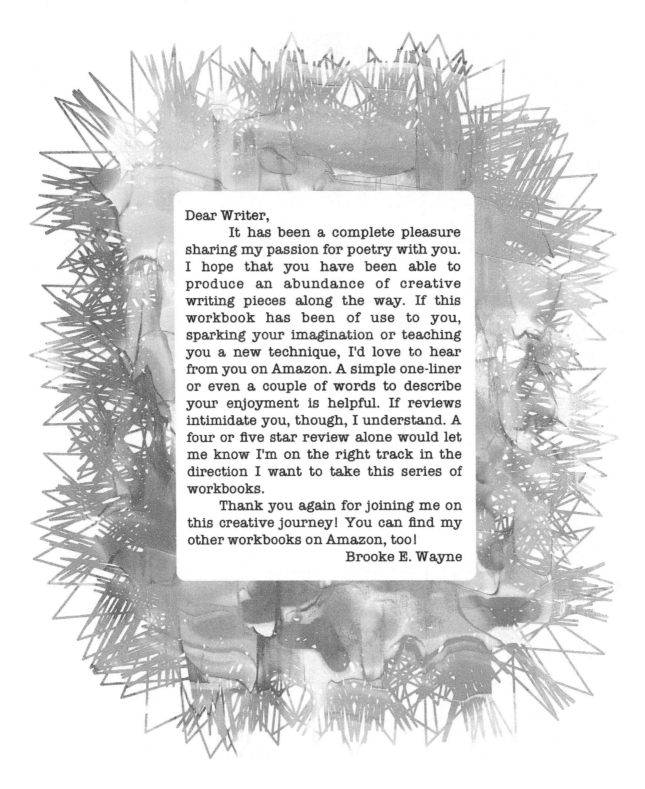

Dear Writer,

It has been a complete pleasure sharing my passion for poetry with you. I hope that you have been able to produce an abundance of creative writing pieces along the way. If this workbook has been of use to you, sparking your imagination or teaching you a new technique, I'd love to hear from you on Amazon. A simple one-liner or even a couple of words to describe your enjoyment is helpful. If reviews intimidate you, though, I understand. A four or five star review alone would let me know I'm on the right track in the direction I want to take this series of workbooks.

Thank you again for joining me on this creative journey! You can find my other workbooks on Amazon, too!

Brooke E. Wayne

How to post a Review: Sign into Amazon. Go to Your Orders. Click on Write a Product Review. It can be as simple as, "I like this workbook because..." or "I recommend this workbook to..."

BROOKE E. WAYNE writes novels for lovers of laughter and romance, giving them an escape from life's hullabaloo. She also produces poetry workbooks to help creative writers sharpen their craft.

Brooke is married to South Philly-born, Eagles-obsessed YouTuber Philly.500, who she met online and fell in love with long before that kind of meet cute was cool. They have two young daughters who flood their happily-ever-after lives with girly giggles and immeasurable love.

Brooke holds a BA in English with a minor in Theology, a MA in Humanities with an emphasis in Literature, two Clear CLAD credentials, and an unofficial PhD in the Art of Snark.

Never without a journal on hand, Brooke has been writing stories and poetry since she was eleven years old. She's had everything from poetry to articles for an encyclopedia set published over the last thirty years. Her romance novels and workbooks are available on Amazon.

When Brooke is not crafting sensual, contemporary romances with lighthearted, witty twists, she teaches English Language Arts, inspiring others to read classic literature and write from the heart.

Brooke E. Wayne

Romance with a Kiss of Humor

WHERE TO FIND THE AUTHOR ONLINE

Website:
http://www.brookeewayne.com

Facebook Page:
https://www.facebook.com/brookeewayne

Instagram:
https://www.instagram.com/authorbrookeewayne

Twitter:
https://www.twitter.com/brookeewayne

Bookbub:
https://www.bookbub.com/profile/brooke-e-wayne

Pinterest:
http://www.pinterest.com/authorbrookeewayne

Publications by
Brooke E. Wayne

CREATIVE WRITING
WORKBOOKS
✦Adults & Teens ✦Tweens & Young Teens ✦Children

✦Poetic Devices ✦Examples ✦Starter Prompts ✦Fill-in-the-Blanks ✦Vocabulary
✦Interactive Experiences ✦Picture Prompts ✦Structured Poems ✦Tips & Tricks

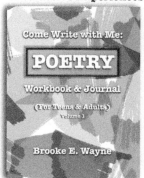 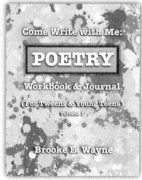 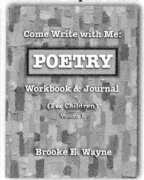

ROMANTIC COMEDY NOVELS

Whine with Cheese (Romantic Comedy Novel)
Love the Wine You're With (Romantic Comedy Novel)
COMING SOON! Wine Not? (Romantic Comedy Novel)

Made in the USA
Middletown, DE
19 June 2024

55998759R00093